Down
For
The
Count

Poetry

G. W. Down

Manor House Publishing Inc.

National Library of Canada
Cataloguing in Publication Data:

Down, G. W.
Down for the Count
Poetry

ISBN: 978-0-9731956-3-7

Copyright 2002-10-15
By G. W. Down.

Published November 15, 2002
by Manor House Publishing
(905) 648-2193

First Edition. 96 pages. 80 poems.
All rights reserved.
Cover Design: G. W. Down/M. B. Davie.
Cover photography: The Corporate Word.
Cover layout/realization: Richard Kosydar.

Acknowledgements

A number of the poems in this book were previously published in *Tower*, a periodical published by the Tower Poetry Society.

'If Not For A Summer's Day' was included in an episode of *Poetry's Alive*, a local cable television programme produced in Hamilton, Ontario in 1984-85.

'Pas De Deux' and 'Native Land' were previously published in *ArtsBeat*, a periodical published by the Hamilton and Region Arts Council.

'Speak To Me, Beloved' was previously published in *Canadian Author*, magazine.

'Basin Head, P.E.I.' was first published in *Tower* in 1986 and later reprinted in *The Eastern Graphic*.

The author expresses his gratitude to Michael B. Davie for the design/layout of this book and to Manor House Publishing Inc. for helping writers' voices to be heard.

- **G. W. Down.**

About the author:

G.W. Down leads a dangerous double life – business executive by day and at other times, a strider on the edges of the after-hours, striking with metaphors at the essence of existence – his true identity known only to a select circle: the readers of his words and verses.

Manor House Publishing Inc.
(905) 648-2193

Dedication:

This book is dedicated to
Readers Everywhere

and
to Trudi,
who throughout our thirty years together,
has made every moment
count as something precious.

Contents

I. GOING DOWN

Melted Dreams
Two
At A Corner
In The Wake Of Remembrance Day
Salad Days, Green In Judgement
To Go Again To Salisbury
Native Land
Black Time
Time Troubled
After The Ten O'clock News
Justice
Game In, Game Out
Police Car
Police Car – Five Years Later
Change
Rebuttal
Choice
In Decision
Grief
The Business Of Lunch
Suitable For Firing
On The Banks Of The Whybash
Suicidal Birds
Man Of The City
In Retirement
Keep The Game Going
If Not For A Summer's Day
Flight To Nowhere
The Line Never Wavered

Lifescape
The Way To School
A Trunkful Of Elephants
Gifts Of Mother
It Isn't Cricket
A Work In Progress
Man To Man
The Release Of Days
One Driving Need Overrides Another
The Company Drift
Basin Head, P.E.I.
The Postcard Province
Newfoundland
When The Price Dropped
Winter Visit To Vancouver
On The Sea-Wall At Stanley Park
Air Water Essence

II. DOWN DEEP

Sudden Arrival
Correction
Pas De Deux
We Play On
The Colour Of An Apple
Rendezvous
Blue To Red
Speak To Me, Beloved
Once And For Always
Beginnings
Not Fallen
Signing The Register
No Time Like The Future
In The Gum-Wood Forest
Tonight, In Our Bedroom

III. THIRD DOWN

September's Blanket
Some Words
For The Record
Death Of The Waves
Nourishment
Hearing Loss
When You Are Away
To Merge With Earth
January By The Lake
Spirit Of The Inland Sea
Lullaby For My Lover
The Image
This Time
Three Falls
Lighten Our Darkness
Perils And Dangers
Of This Night
The February 24th Sleep Experience
The Match

Foreword

G. W. Down is a rare talent – as I discovered during a Christmas party of the Tower Poetry Society.

As a publisher/author, I was one of the guests milling about the Dundas home of a fellow poet.

Within moments, I had the pleasure of chatting with G. W. Down as we competed for the dwindling supply of snacks on the kitchen table.

Noticing his reach, and the fact that we were both eyeing the same, lone, peanut-butter cookie, I decided to distract the man by expressing an interest in his poetry.

Not that I wasn't otherwise interested in his poems: But securing a tasty cookie was the more pressing matter at hand.

G. W. – I can call him that, as we're close – happily discussed his poems while I listened quite attentively and munched on the cookie.

I was already familiar with his work from reading Tower Poetry Society publications. But the cookie was delicious – and G. W. was on a roll.

Besides, some of his newest poems sounded quite intriguing.

I expressed an interest in reading more of his poetry and he followed through on his promise to send me a collection of his poems.

Quite seriously, on receiving his poetic offering, I was impressed with the clarity and imagery incorporated in his writing.

That clarity came to a brief, crashing halt when I happened to peruse the About-The-Author bio information I'd requested. This cryptic bit of subterfuge presents more questions than answers – perhaps he's building a mystery. Frankly, on reading the About-The-Author bio, I don't even know where he's from. I think he's a local poet. But I'm not sure.

That said, on reading his poems, it became clear right away that this is a gifted poet. He effortlessly draws the reader deep inside the moods and places he creates.

And there are gems throughout this book, that frankly, I'm very proud to have published.

His poem: Lifescape combines the image of a fresh canvas with a return to youth and a rekindled willingness to experience a new beginning while denying the inevitable end.

In The Gum-Wood Forest, another poem, is rich with the imagery of a musty nature captured in a library/den with "leather-bound leaves on oaken shelves bearing the fruit of countless minds gathered…"

His poem: To Go Again to Salisbury, in fact, takes you to Salisbury to sip "dry wine when we meet," and to walk among the "towering Sentinel rocks on Salisbury's plain."

Rendezvous, another poem, tells of a private meeting between lovers who "feed their spirits until they sleep within their cocoon of cathedral skies with the sweet wine still upon their lips…"

I know what you're thinking: That's the second reference to wine. And we have a back cover picture of G. W. about to down a goblet!

But it's all poetic licence. There's no danger we'll have to rush G. W. to AA, ASAP.

So drink deeply of his poems. He's pouring.

- **Michael B. Davie,** publisher/author, Winning Ways.

DOWN FOR THE COUNT

G. W. Down

Manor House Publishing Inc.
(905) 648-2193

I.

GOING DOWN

MELTED DREAMS

The melted dreams of yesterday
Are fuel for the fire
That burns with flame so strong to form
The next day's proud desire;
Thus, deep within the crucible
Of time, life, age and youth,
The old wants with the new will fuse,
Still searching for the truth.

TWO

Guilty as charged was the jury's call
For the man with the murderous past;
My body's my own was the mother's cry,
Give me leave to go to the clinic.

Impassioned pleas to show compassion
Prevailed on the government's conscience;
The convicted man was pardoned at ten,
The innocent died at midnight.

AT A CORNER

Behind the brick-faced bushes
Near the wilderness of choice
Lurked the self-named defender
Of the sanctity of life.
Crouched righteous for the advent
Of the birthright foe, he spied
His prey of clinic-keepers,
Sprang civilized to the crowd,
Patted his automatic
Soothing messenger of truth,
Pulled it from its pocket womb
And opened fire.

IN THE WAKE OF REMEMBRANCE DAY

They fought the obvious enemy
Which swept across chromatic freedom,
Obliterating level borders
In a jealous open tide of fear,
Propelled by overbearing guile and
Zealous creed of genetic destiny.

We must contend with a subtler foe
That worms its way into coded laws,
That would erode everything they won,
Hacking into presumed innocence
To programme seizure without arrest,
Trial without court, penalty without proof.

It denigrates opposed opinion,
Sponges away the qualms of conscience –
An enemy without and within;
Let there be balance in our vision,
Let there be reasoning in our thoughts,
Lest we sleep dreamless through the next attack.

SALAD DAYS, GREEN IN JUDGEMENT

Peach thrills anew
To the gift of life,
The memory
Of its blossom days
Bobbing with it in the morning breeze.

Rhubarb squats stolidly
On the flat ground,
Its second season coming;
Experienced, it knows the terrors of life
And the pain of lost appendages.

Sunshine on garden soil is a siren's call
As lettuce surges skyward,
Proudly pushing back the mighty earth,
Exuberant youth in every leaf
Bursting to trumpet a song of joy.

But hush now!
Try to be brave,
Attempt to endure,
To calm the tremors and control the screams
As a vegetarian approaches.

TO GO AGAIN TO SALISBURY

Dry wine when we meet,
From an empty automatic press,
An embrace of ice,
Cold as the nave of that ancient cathedral
Where the Great Charter
Of our shared life was sealed long ago
When I did not dream
Love could ever be entombed.

Is it light or lack
Thereof that tints your eyes to such dull grey?
Oh that I could draw
The blue back into your eyes by deft brush-strokes,
And caress your brow
To its erstwhile shimmering lustre
That lifted spirits
As the floodlights lift and float that tall church-spire.

It was our church-spire
When we strolled through its grounds in our honeyed
                                      month,
Before stone silent
Barriers obtruded in our midst,
Origin unknown,
To preside over love's slow decay
Like the towering
Sentinel rocks on Salisbury's plain.

We owned all the world
When we had nothing but ourselves
And the face of hope
For long bright years together.
Perhaps cathedrals
Resurrection-sites may be; if we return
Love may rise once more —
Can we go there again?

NATIVE LAND

Skilful hands began to plant the factories,
Other braves sowed the seeds of machinery;
Sinuous warriors danced up rain pollution,
Overt hunters captured fossil fuels.

Forget about your claims for compensation,
The owl knows when nests are past repair;
The eagle keeps his eye upon the future,
The beaver builds a house from broken trees.

BLACK TIME

White swallows black and you're raucous,
Raging, refusing to trade;
Time for a change, is your focus,
Time that the payment was made.

Black snuffs out black and you're silent,
Stridently holding your place;
It isn't a matter of darkness,
It isn't a problem of race.

TIME TROUBLED

Oh I am worn and wrinkled
As I peer into my glass,
And trace the tracks the crow has left
To score the years that pass.

Time now leaves an ugly press
On my bruised and broken frame;
This stooped, slow-moving, humbled form
Will never be the same.

Youthful plans to win the world
Gave way to lesser vision,
Great grand schemes were narrowed down
To paths of more precision.

What have years of weary trudge
Achieved towards my ambition?
The shrieking winds gasp for breath,
All screaming in derision.

Strands of empty shorelines swept
By breakers lie behind me,
Sands wiped clean of any mark:
No follower could find me.

But doubts can fade to purple
In the early twilight hours,
Chased into the shadows by
My few remaining powers.

All has edged to this one point,
All that's left revolves about
The need to leave some lasting deed
Before the tide goes out.

AFTER THE TEN O'CLOCK NEWS

Spare us, Uncle,
Not another tiresome tirade
On the great eternal mystery
Of men not learning
Anything from history.

We too well know the past mistakes
Of our fellow human souls,
And we could counsel them, we know,
Were they now here,
Not six below.

There is not one of us who, from the shore,
Could not dam a river's course,
Yet the swimmer caught by undertow
Can but strive against the current,
Cannot stop the flow.

No, not one here who cannot solve
The maze and find
The riddle's gate
For all events
Save those in which we now participate.

JUSTICE

She was blindfolded in her prime,
Eyes cleared from the distorting smiles
And grimaces, the contrived dress
Cloaking deceptive supplicants
Who charmed and courted for redress.

Handsome liars were forced to press
Their claims in logical debate.
But now she stares out open-eyed
At videos and cameras
While balanced wisdom's pushed aside.

GAME IN, GAME OUT

Should not little boys play cowboys?
Parents loathe such violent games;
A generation weaned on cap-guns
Grew to shun the sight of bloodshed,
Now the Indian wins.

As the human race leaps forward
Youngsters play at space invaders,
Zap whole planets to oblivion
With the flicker of an eyelid
In the name of progress.

POLICE CAR

The black and white has turned to yellow;
Is this the fading of all ages?
Has justice withered like old parchment
Brittle from the press of hopeless years,
An archaic concept past its prime,
An elder monarch in failing health?

Or is it jaundice, symptomatic
Of a bilious indigestion
All the citizens are forced to bear?
The urban liver's vital functions
Cannot cleanse the entire system
Nor store a nutrient sweet enough.

Yellow once was the colour of fear;
Perhaps patrols have yielded power
To the set that brooks no arm of law,
That dreads displays of strength of purpose.
Were the black and white too starkly drawn?
Too much clarity, too intensive?

POLICE CAR — FIVE YEARS LATER

To gain a greater recognition
Pervasive white replaces yellow,
A contract bleaching primed and aimed to
Sweep out colour and reflect all light.
This pristine coat you sport is set to
Sum the spectrum within your precincts,
Arrest the eye on your successes
And conceal the darkness drawn along.

Yet your side reveals a snatch of blue;
Was that some artist's inattention?
Or do you hesitate to deny
Impurity, and seek to soften
Your dazzle by addition of a touch
Of ice, a hint of melancholy?
You carry as well a dash of red —
A mark of health, but is it also
Warning against too much exertion?
Is your commission's makeup traced by
Your periodic changes of face?
What paint will you wear five years from now?

CHANGE

Gauge your steps before you take them
Nor advance while too uncertain,
See effects before you make them
Else is change the final curtain.

REBUTTAL

Many branches cannot be seen
When a path is first in vision,
The place one holds may seem serene
But they survive who change position.

CHOICE

To note what's wrong, must be removed,
And not to fear ideas strange;
But history has quite disproved
The notion everything should change.

IN DECISION

Lost in thought without a road map,
No known route to open action —
Stymied by imponderables,
Stunned by pressing abstract questions,
The scanner strains for throughway words.

Missing signs for the express lane
And clutching now at catch-phrases
The planner spins to side-track paths,
Veers off soft shoulders to become
In inconclusive prattle mired.

A nettled navigator prompts
The necessary reversal,
The long roll back to new designs,
The measured tread of tireless
Ideas lined in solid planes.

GRIEF

You wear your spectacles loosely
So you can read the world at will;
For now your angel's footsteps have vanished,
But you believe you hear her still.
Why do you persist in tracing
Shadows in the park,
When many need your beacon
To thread the needling creeping dark?
A child without a hand
Has no strength left to stand.

THE BUSINESS OF LUNCH

One little - two little - three manhattans
Chase the ritualistic exchange of cards;
Neglected menus languish pining
By orphaned bread-and-butter plates.
Food defers while sharks go fishing;
Conversation takes a tap-dance
Round tables of percentage, prime,
Dollars and no sense,
Adequacy of rate,
Efficacy of reserve,
A host of other subjects that deserve
The homage of the guests assembled.
Hawk and hawker warily spar,
Seeking, probing, nodding, shaking,
Trading glances, measuring chances,
Searching for a common ground.

Three-quarters time has suddenly vanished;
Systems growl an urgent message
That breakfast was eaten an aeon ago,
And a junior aide seizes the moment
To bark to the servers to bring his reward.
Orders are hasty, fourth cocktails are quick;
Waiters conduct their deals with cunning,
Moving in when demand is anxious,
Stepping out when supply is high.
Mouths which lately spoke all hollow
Fill with rare untasted feast;
Knife and fork are frenzied flashes,
Jab for profit, cut at cost,
Appropriate the assets fast;
Declining stock is swallowed swiftly
To rouse from slumber ulcers, angry.

Minor officials who'd prefer calm chewing
Must pace with the man who'll be paying the bill;
With splashes of coffee and smiles of thanks
The members rise for their next appointments, late.
Small matter no bargain was struck today,
That was not the meeting's foremost intent:
All are aware that the business of lunch
Is allowing the parties
To see one another
In an easy, relaxing environment.

SUITABLE FOR FIRING

Gnarled, twisted, defiant,
Obstinate, unyielding
To all saws,
Not even fit for trim,
You crouch on combed earth and
Flaunt your flaws.
You never could have been
A chair, for you have not
Couth enough;
You might have made a board
But it needs much more than
Being tough.
No desk for you, nor will
You fill a door except
In exit;
Oh dull and senseless block,
The axe will fall on you —
No respite!
Black will be your finish
When your termination
Is required;
Cold weather marks your end —
One strike, and come winter
You'll be fired.

ON THE BANKS
OF THE WHYBASH

They gush glibly about
Customer service
Even as they hurtle
Their compatriots,
Their domestic clients,
Into a rapids of
Ever-rising charges —
Fees for drafts, for current balance,
Fees no less to make deposit,
To splash the fund of liquid assets;
And while the banks yet gorge on fees
Their swollen stream of crushing profits
Rushes on to lend its force
To large misshapen leveraged buyouts —
Dug from plans in shallow pools —
Already flung beyond control
And struggling now to stay afloat.
On and on that stream keeps surging,
Headed next for foreign waters
To revere the global tribute aerie
Perched aloft by swimming minds
Heedless of defaulted nations,
Oblivious to eroded credit,
Bent instead toward turgid trade.
Those atop the crests of banks,
Fattened by their creamy pay-scales,
Bask in torpor on the rocks.
All this cash outflow disquiets,
Rips the life from retired folk,
Drains the salt from honest labour,
Kills the seed of intelligent growth.

SUICIDAL BIRDS

Poised to avoid the long flight south
They wheel and rush at speedy trucks,
Or loiter on the asphalt soil
To stare and dare all sporty vans;
They linger in a rising swing
Or hop across a hot rod's path;
They swoop to block a pick-up's route
Or dance in front of sleek sedans.

Can they not judge the thrusts of wind?
Their scatter-patterned failed escape
Suggests they were not taught the moves
To aim away from looming grilles.
They've too much trust in human brakes —
Or do they choose to self-destruct?
It's only fools and fledglings who
Chase after thrills with too few skills.

MAN OF THE CITY

An ancient tribal instinct gnaws his nerves,
Reminding him he has an open flank;
The home he left this morning still preserves
Its quiet calm, its honest face so frank,
That speaks of labour earning comfort there,
Where no degree of lock or theft alarm
Is adequate to make one less the ware
Of threat of vandals, thugs and other harm.
And when his woman goes about the streets
Will she be safe from greedy piercing eyes?
Must she mistrust each stranger that she meets,
Examine every phrase for covert lies?
The city gathers in its troubled clay
And struggles through another frightened day.

IN RETIREMENT

How appropriate, a golden watch
For watching all the seconds
Of all the days
Of what are blithely called
The Golden Years.

This timepiece has a numbered face
Much like mine with its measured markings;
The difference is,
When my hour is up
I'll have not the luxury to go round again.

Waterproof —
I'm said to be some seventy-five percent
Composed of that compound,
So I doubt I'm bothered by water,
Except that what man is
That it is which destroys him.
Stainless steel back —
Yes, there's a brace
I'll be forced to wear.
Shockproof, too —
I have that feature,
There's little left that could jolt me now.
Dustproof —
Ah, now there I differ,
For I will surely yield to dust
And not be proof against myself.
Self-winding, guaranteed
To last a lifetime —
I too make that idle boast;
I've been winding up
As long as I've been living
And what is a lifetime but that which one lasts?

KEEP THE GAME GOING

Keep the game going,
Deal the cards again,
Let me bar the daybreak
From this night of pain.

I was dealt in king,
Soon turned to a knave;
Heart came after diamonds,
Much too late to save.

Aims have gone amiss,
Not the way I planned;
Playing without feeling,
I have lost the hand.

Deal me not a spade,
Deal some other ace;
Light comes after darkness,
Light that I can't face.

Many clubs have come,
Many players gone;
I know all the rules here,
Nothing else beyond.

So keep the game going,
Deal the cards again,
Let me bar the daybreak
From this night of pain.

IF NOT FOR A SUMMER'S DAY

If not for a summer's day
One would think all time had ceased,
Since the fall winter spring are
An endless procession of grief;
And the light in her eyes was
A rainbow; a mischievous thief
Was her smile, stealing my sight
And my mind — not my heart, which
Always belonged in summer
With you. Now the fall winter spring
Grow a grey garden round me,
For time is a pitiless thing.

FLIGHT TO NOWHERE

She wore the suit of vaunted nothingness,
With blank face and hypodermic-pocked arm.
Ringed by thrall and bloused in self-absorption
She glazed through halls she thought she danced, 'til a
Door slammed and terror crept through the keyhole
To jacket her world with shapeless colour.
Nameless tones collided with her hearing;
She swirled in the skirt of brimming floodlight,
Drummed by a distant moaning, emptily
Indiscernible from her surroundings,
Cast among the spirit fragments, senses
Fugitive and screaming for the return.

THE LINE NEVER WAVERED

When I was young the line was clear;
No one wondered, no one doubted,
We knew no quandary of right
Or wrong, the truth was silver pure —
And the line never wavered.

Mathematics taught me asymptotes,
Hyperbolas, parabolas;
Ideas range in wider arcs
As the mind becomes less finite —
Still the line never wavered.

Crime and justice were not functions
Of remote mislaid equations;
Mercy often tempered judgement,
Yet guilt was not unrecognized —
And the line never wavered.

But that was all too long ago;
Different years have left their tread,
Confusing markers mar the path,
Vision's blurred, the route's obscured —
And the line is scarcely visible.

LIFESCAPE

Let me return
To the art studio of my youth,
And be again fresh canvas
Waiting for the play of colours,
Free from the frames
That pronounce completion,
Ready for tinges and splashes
To enrich the pattern.

This visit may provide time
To erase errant strokes,
To change dark shades
That point to darker corners,
To brighten hues
That heighten understanding,
To alter the elements
Being gathered for the gallery,
To deny the inevitability
Of the collection's final composition.

THE WAY TO SCHOOL

Off to school, midwinter morning,
With easy strides at eight years old,
I do not mind the press of clothes
Nor care about the climate.

Little Susan, hair like sunrise,
Lives along my route two blocks,
Little Susan, lofty cheekbones,
Struggling against a bully's blows.

No marksman I, no strength of arm,
But Passion lends me power,
And Fury lifts my leaden hand
While Justice weights my aim.

A snowball volley follows next,
A two-fisted fusillade,
A startled cry, a crack of slush
Smack in the bully's face.

Her assailant stops, wipes his chin
And flees the scene of battle;
Little Susan, eyes of fawn,
Embraces her new champion.

Little Susan's grateful smile
Is a galaxy of pearls;
Her fawns grow impish, twinkling
At her playful toss of snow.

So now there is no help for it,
It cannot be avoided;
No second thoughts can change my fate,
I shall be late for school again.

A TRUNKFUL OF ELEPHANTS

My father had a herd of elephants
Ranged along his mantel,
Pachyderms of porcelain
Arrayed to view the doorway,
To greet his friends and bring good luck
And guard his castle's safety.

In time so many elephants he had
That some were put away,
Out of sight but not forgotten,
Stored for later days.
He placed the others on a shelf,
They boldly faced the clock.

Tough and solid, large of heart,
Unswaying when bearing burdens,
Immensely strong, yet gentle too,
Quiet and good-natured,
Occasionally sparkling
When trumpeting good causes-

So he was to all who knew him
And they, like the elephants,
Shall never forget.

GIFTS OF MOTHER

Her gifts were gifts of nurturing comfort,
From gentle warmth, a prescient healing
Foreseeing needs before they were expressed,
But not constrictive, never congealing.

How smooth the folds of precise-trimmed paper
And creased with care so creases lie hidden —
Unselfish parcel, brought to offer calm
Solicitude and prayers unbidden.

She would take pains to package the present
In brightest colours, ribbon slenderest,
And truly every gift she ever gave
Was wrapped in love and tagged with tenderness.

A WORK IN PROGRESS

A child is not a blank page
On which are to be photocopied
All the whims and prejudices
Of judgemental elders,
But a novel half finished,
Already encoded with
Subtleties of text and
Tangled nests of sub-plots.
There must be characters of principle
But the story must find purpose;
Like every work in progress
It must explore and examine options,
Not be bound in by
Predetermined expectations.

IT ISN'T CRICKET
HOW THE MIGHTY ARE FALLEN IN MID-SEASON

A gallant cricketer,
Last term's college hero,
Has been laid low
By a prefect
From the sister school;
A stunning beauty, she bowled him out
In one over
At a recent get-acquainted tea.

No pop-fly this,
Nor leg before,
But a cleanly smitten wicket.
The batsman left his crease,
Saw no hope
Of his salvation;
Toward her, his heart's treasure,
He has with one run declared.

Now his mid-week match
Is a true test,
As he endures valiantly,
Knowing she is near the pitch,
Waiting for the tea-break,
His time with her.

When fielding, he was silly mid-on,
But missed so many catches

By looking in her direction
That now he's slips
And watches the wicket-keeper's back.
Even there his gaze may stray
And to the captain's dismay
Too many balls slip past the slips.

His game's so badly off,
They may try him at mid-off,
Or perhaps put him
Off the field entirely;
But that would suit him well,
For since he has a girl-friend
He'd prefer to be
The scorer.

MAN TO MAN

The pain is at once chronic and acute,
The biceps rebel at emptiness when
Embracing the vestiges of a man,
Holding shoulders that have shrunk to fibrils.

But in the mind's reach those shoulders are broad
As when they tossed a trembling four-year-old
To the sky, and those knees are still as strong
As when they bounced a joyful six-year-old.

That abdominal oedema invades
The eyes and swells all four lacrimal ducts;
Like its failing heart, that concave chest droops
After more than six months of suffering.

Those hands grasp the aching fingers tightly,
With assurance, shaking solid welcome;
Comes that voice, robust in recognition —
And pain dissolves like dew in the morning.

THE RELEASE OF DAYS

The shell staged its exit:
A plate of teeth, a cloudy eye,
A blackened gangrenous foot;
Like a snake shedding skin,
A ship jettisoning cargo,
His departure was piecemeal.
Size of cells diminished;
A cough compressed his breath until
Disencumbered he flew forth.

ONE DRIVING NEED
OVERRIDES ANOTHER

Above the line of traffic vision
Is where full wonderment bides, but still
It would be to court catastrophe
To let attention be diverted
From white striped links on the black sinew
To stare in awe at the stippled red
And spaniel grey in the sunset sky
With turquoise patch where the brow nods up
And crimson swirl where the night shifts in.

THE COMPANY DRIFT

Feeble commanders flip charts to change course
With fixed inconstancy,
Ordering their stars by the crests and troughs
Of evanescent thought;
Able-minded men navigate blandly
In apathy's compass,
Measuring their careers in time left
Until retirement;
Skilful fashioners ply their craft tightly,
Tacked in narrow vision,
Moored to the mainframe, trading purpose for
Channelled activity.
Officers flounder, juggle their sheets and
Rail at receding tides;
Lashed by the fear of falling overboard,
Ensigns steer in a fog.
Power of motion is gone, and willing
Hands stand empty of hope;
Crew members watch and pray for storms to break
This terrifying calm.

BASIN HEAD, P.E.I.

North of the mouse's nest,
Where red soil weds white sand,
And gleeful children jump
With yelps of young pleasure
Off an aged bridge to
A ripe brook seaward-bound,
Where grave adolescents
Reassuringly teach
Non-swimmers and block their
Hooligan tormentors,
At that warm place we paused,
And watched waves of sunshine
Blend the grey of wisdom
With ardent blossom pink;
Mix of generations
Prospers there forever.
To those who would freeze time,
Let it be known that it
Is daily done and done
With ease at Basin Head.

THE POSTCARD PROVINCE

Snapshot trail of empty revelation:
The postcard province, which applauds itself
In excessive misdirected ardour,
Boasts in brimming self-congratulation
Two-way rapids, pseudo-magnetism
And a ghost-ship in the Baie des Chaleurs.

Such limited fancies make little more
Than duty junkets on the journey east,
An interruption on the highway to
Digby's scallops or Truro's tidal bore.
Lost is other print behind the picture,
Being not the usual tourist hue.

Staking out the first stamp of this province,
Villages grew up by sanguine rivers,
From the stream in columns fields retreated.
Like windblown fog progress made its entrance,
Marched its company store up to the bank;
Quiet village life appeared defeated.

Forests line the roads for leagues of silence,
Scribbled notes tell the past's place of hiding;
Farm and factory share one bivouac
In a shifting, picturesque alliance
As deceptive as the hill at Moncton,
Elusive as a phantom schooner's tack.

NEWFOUNDLAND

It is often difficult
To get to Newfoundland;
Too many times
The ferries do not ply
And aeroplanes are grounded
Or re-routed.
It has always been the case:
One must strive for one's Heart's Desire,
And Paradise
Is not easily attained;
One comes by effort, not by chance
To Heart's Content.
Yet well should one persevere:
Riches reward the struggle
To reach the rock;
The breath, imperilled by rugged
Topography, is restored
By magic charm.
Time drums a hardy rhythm
Where weather is uncertain;
Not waiting for
Fine days that may not come, they
Plant flowers in the pelting rain
In Newfoundland.
This province is the drawing-room
Where hospitality was invented;
Camaraderie spreads its warmth
And every home is a Solarium.
Mainland cares are zones distant;
Reason beckons me to
Remain longer;
Were it possible I would
Delay departure far more than
Half an hour.

WHEN THE PRICE DROPPED

We walked as in a dream
Through the Alberta city's bosom;
Once it had heaved
With the mighty breath of action,
Now it barely stirred,
So soft and slight its movement.
The city showed no vestige
Of its former heat,
Its temporal pulse so weak
The beat was almost imperceptible.

Gone was the gush
Of teeming throbbing commerce;
Left behind were
The gleaming glassy buildings
Tall enough to scratch the clouds
And start the rain of disillusion.
Not Sunday morning,
But midweek noon
In an almost empty civic well,
Where sudden wealth was turned to worry,
With energy drained from magnates' faces
And half the influx drawn back east.
But later, over dinner,
The Albertans talked of
Everything but blackness.
They ranged the country's length and breadth,
And then their topics stretched and spanned the
                                      globe;
They spoke of hopes and longings universal,
They evinced a permanence,
A refinement pure enough
To prove again humanity
Is fuelled by more than oil.

WINTER VISIT TO VANCOUVER

By three hours' time we were a world away;
While Niagara nestled in white driven
Lattices of clouds' cream amid cold cut rock
We roamed in shirt-sleeves and watched boaters basking
In the grey aftermath of a rain-dulled day.

They thrive in a winter playground warm and bland.
What is to savour of the thrust of mountains
Or the lie of storied parks in starless sleep
Mired, when the time is neither green nor icy?
What will expand the soul when spring makes its stand?

Can there be pleasure at the first vernal jump
If it be from a depth so mediocre?
What joy brings July if December lacks grit?
Pity Vancouver six months hence, tanned, ensconced
On summer's hump, but not primed by winter's pump.

ON THE SEA-WALL AT STANLEY PARK

Wrapped in the spandex throttle of motion,
Driven by the drab motive of self-shape,
Heedless of the grandeur that surrounds them,
Puffing a broken-steam-engine track-scrape,
The joggers erupt in arrhythmic ash
Jerking along the measured Saturday matin,
Tumbling toward the destined cigarette
Or brewed palliative or caffeine mash.

Pedestrians in their path take more care,
Twirling the facets of jewelled nature's vision
Through all their senses, carat by carat
To catch memories from the lustrous air.
They drink the majesty of pearl mountain
Rinsing its health in shade marine blue-grey,
Climb the reflection of look-out station,
And glide the aqua expansive walkway.

AIR   WATER   ESSENCE

The breeze blows softly for refreshment
Or the wind forms power for the sail;
The dew cleanses worn grass and flowers
Or rain coaxes produce from the soil;
The fog poses questions for the brain
Or the sun heats hunger in the soul.

II.

DOWN DEEP

SUDDEN ARRIVAL

Winter's departure was premature;
We were ill-prepared for the springtime
Which caromed off the north and bounded
Into being before the snow had
Cooled our heads and cleansed our grounds.
Startled from our hibernation
We could not blink and search for shadows
Nor cling to the safety of long night.
Your warmth was devastating as it
Crushed the frost, released ophthalmic flood.

CORRECTION

We were wrong at dinner the other night:
We had it backwards;
A mistake so easy to make, yet I
Saw it afterwards.
If you re-examine the ways of each,
You too will soon see
What's now clear to me:
He's brilliant, but she's a genius.

PAS DE DEUX

Exasperating exertion,
To make the forehead rivers run
And make me swallow my own sweat
In the heat of firewood splits.
She cups a splashed invitation,
Pours liquid down her sleek bronzed throat
In hurried quaff that thrusts out air
But cannot douse a blazing thirst.
From ageless lapping motion
The shoreline lips its mound of earth,
Then the primal waters beckon
And we are awash in rebirth.

WE PLAY ON

We play on, though my part staggers
In our discordant duet:
An aging, strained autumnal man
Clutching corrosive desire,
Groping for elusive fire,
Grimly drifting toward winter —
No match for your springtime vigour.

Now as you approach ecstasy
I trail behind and pull you back,
Raging at expired rhythm,
Thrashing in the sudden quiet;
But you disrupt this fugue, sighing
With warmth and draw me toward you
And we begin to play anew.

THE COLOUR OF AN APPLE

Red
    as the cherry cheeks of healthy youth
      the bridal blush of innocence
      the blood of pulsing passion

Green
    as untutored steps of novices
      the strengthening gait of spring
      the steady grace of rainfall

Yellow
    as the jagged fear of failure
      the level sun at mid-day
      the light of growing knowledge

Brown
    when intrusive air bruises the opened sphere
    and hopes to spoil the deepest essence

Gold
    not as the prize of Aphrodite
    but as the element that glistens
        the value that endures

RENDEZVOUS

In the anonymity of night
He moves, where intrusive glares are far
And harmless; she sets his fire by
The whispering waters, and they talk
And dream and warm their flesh,
Feed their spirits,
Until they sleep within their cocoon
Of cathedral skies
With the sweet wine still upon their lips.
Before morning when the sun and wind
Can burn again,
She is restored and he is strengthened.

BLUE TO RED

By the wink of an eye
She turns my mood from blue to red,
Firing the mind,
Quickening the pulse,
Freshening the blood —
An oxygenation of the soul.

SPEAK TO ME, BELOVED

Spin out your thoughts in streaming rhythmic beats;
To emotions give elaboration,
Gilt tones to the pounding from your soul.

Suspend your clipped speech.

I will have none of your sparse fragments;
I want to hear your mind exhaled
And etched in wondrous rounded musings.

ONCE AND FOR ALWAYS

The park was trimmed in the signature of winter.
Cold sloped from the west, ribboned and unremitting,
Borne on a northern-quartered rising loop of wind.
Failing sunlight pawed the frosted earthen matting;
Trailing rays stole past coniferous sentinels
To stroke the line of brush in leeward clearing pinned.

Snowflakes, fingerprints of the clouds — no two alike —
Arrayed themselves to press the frame of this moment,
In powdered whorl to stamp it with a permanence
Which rolling tempering seasons cannot erase.
Braced by their air of perpetual flowing ease
We shyly touched, then joined our hands with confidence.

Precious hours stand alone, float through time
                                          — pushed past,
But not swamped by the crushing blot of change, nor to
Be duplicated, even by couples who deign
To spell a future from a single glowing scene.
We kissed and began our love, engulfed in the weld
Of what can ever be and never be again.

BEGINNINGS

We shall have many new beginnings,
And each shall usher in a thousand
Lifetimes' worth of lasting happiness
And love.

Each new morning and every evening
Shall spotlight limits undiscovered;
Each time I lift your hand to my lips
To kiss
The touch that presses dreams to motion,
And pour my soul into your cup of
Replenishing spirit, health to drink
Anew,

At all such times I shall remember:
Before you there was but existence,
The beginning of beginnings was
With you.

NOT FALLEN

We did not fall in love, you and I —
We were elevated into it;
We vaulted across its foremost step
Deliberately wholeheartedly
Embracing the consequences of
Escalation of our affection.

Confident assurance guided us;
There was no question of whether love
Would endure, no uncertainty to
Our upward path, nothing frightening.
One does not start a steep ascent nor
Proceed but with a trusted partner.

How did such trust arise between us?
Admiration bloomed observing acts
Which sprang from warm limbs of joy and grace;
A divine beneficence blesses
Those who bless and cleanse the world with love;
All other factors do not matter.

SIGNING THE REGISTER

Such soft and delicate hands you have –
Doll's hands, as my father said –
Yet what strength they contain, to harness
The hope of a grand future
And grasp it firmly tamed in a pen;
You write your name beside mine
And our lives combine in that signing.
You place your small hand in mine
And we each hold the world and, joined, hold
More than the world, enough that
Nothing is beyond our reach as we
Proceed forth into the world.

NO TIME LIKE THE FUTURE

Time, it is said, is what permits
Beginnings and endings.

For us and our love
There was surely a beginning
But it can scarcely be recalled;
So pervasive is our love
And so entrenched that its origins
Are not easily traced.

There are milestones which mark
The continuation of our passion;
There are seasons and anniversaries
Now measurable by dozens
And seemingly destined
To be counted by hundreds and more,
To overwhelm the notion
Of finite numbers.

We face a limitless vista
Stretching beyond sight
Beyond imagination
To what cannot be called
A termination;
Come, have no fear of endings.

Let us process into
This boundless future
That defies its own definition,
Being itself timeless.

IN THE GUM-WOOD FOREST

At fireside in the gum-wood forest
With its leather-bound leaves on oaken shelves
Bearing the fruit of countless minds gathered,
We clasp and share the stories of ourselves.

You curl your fingers against the phrases;
I read flourishing passion and joy by
Scanning your laughter, light as the crack of
The stone-fringed flame beside your blazing eyes.

In solitude we wrap hearts together,
The timbre of voices softens and dips;
Tender low tones dance back from the shadows,
Bathed in the breath from your nourishing lips.

TONIGHT, IN OUR BEDROOM

The universe reunified
And all its disparate components
Recoiled into one elemental
Recombinant mass.

Everything of matter merged and
Blended into one surpassing spring
While the traits and styles of each remained
Recognized and loved.

Rescued from the clutches of time
Two souls braved frontiers of a new plane,
Followed arcs of an expanding orb,
Glimpsed infinity.

III.

THIRD DOWN

SEPTEMBER'S BLANKET

September's blanket
Has little to do with fallen leaves;
They bide their time to shape
A crisp October crust —
But in September the cover
Comes from sudden gusty chills,
The face of autumn peeking in
At bedroom windows,
Misty breath to cool
The edge of steaming sheets.

September is a cold compress
To soothe the fevered summer forehead,
As well an antidote
To languid sultry lethargy;
It is a curtain
Dropping down on easy August scenes,
A shroud that darkly
Smothers thriving summer passion,
And a protection
Against too much happiness.

SOME WORDS

Some words, beautiful before voiced,
Delightful to the brimming heart,
Are too treacherous for the lung;
Awkward and unsteady mixtures,
They are perilous, and may prove
A mine-field for the teeth and tongue.
Caution cannot cure their nature;
Such words should die in the mind's eye.

FOR THE RECORD

Bless us, Father, for we can no longer confess
                                       our sins.

The last confession was ten strokes ago.

The nature of the sins is such that
No one dare admit guilt
Or offer contrition.

There are cries of blood for faults acknowledged,
The plea becomes confounded
And one wrong grows to legion
In the race to place blame Somewhere
Anywhere
To lash at Someone
Anyone...

The innocent stand suspected;
The guilty live with burdens unremitting,
No receipt for payment made in full.

Sickness wins no mercy in such climate;
The cured are hounded in the trap of their release,
They hear the breath of heaving backyard
                                       neighbours,
They brush the dust of urban hatred blocks.

I cannot talk to my lawyer —
That confidentiality has already
Been compromised;
And physicians' files can be warranted open
To judiciary eyes;

And this, this last place of sanctuary
Will be next.

My crime is in speaking against all this.

What you have here is the truth
And nothing but the truth –
But not the whole truth.
Did ever any earthly court,
With its barbed and limited searches,
Elicit all knowledge
And hear the whole truth?

I will go and say no more.

Nor should you hear one word further.
Take this to the police, and quickly –
Before they come to question you,
Before they can detain you,
Before they accuse you –

For they will accuse you:
Of withholding evidence,
Of closing the door
So as to keep vengeance out
And let justice in –
Serious charges, Father,
And you will be tried.

Go quickly, please.

DEATH OF THE WAVES

When the sun rides high and the water churns
And the wind never pauses for breath,
The sparkles gather and smile at the terns
While the waves chase the foam to their death.

They surge like the boldest warrior hawks
For they seek a most glorious end,
Caressing the sand and slapping the rocks,
The mundane and the drear to transcend.

They desire to die with their spray ablaze
In their catapult high on the shore,
Distinguished and proud and ending their days
Once they've passed through oblivion's door.

But they shall be cheated in this perverse
Vain attempt to be lastingly squashed;
So soon they strike they'll be caused to reverse
And coast back from the land where they washed.

They will find that crashing altered their aim
And their consciousness level is new;
Experienced energy knows no frame,
Squares its course whence its mass first withdrew.

The waves back through limitless vistas sigh,
Past markers both familiar and strange,
To track through destiny's storm to the eye –
Yes a death's but a quickening change.

NOURISHMENT

Droop-eyed and drawn taut
From insufficient sleep,
I watch while you take
Nourishment through a needle
And tour the nightingale corridors
Past the charts of warded vigilance
And the cells of antisepsis.

Nutrient in solution
From plastic mass on a toted pole
Salts away the problem
Of mortal sustenance
When nothing by mouth is permitted,
And days stretch out to following days
In exercise of healing.

You are steeped in sutures, but I perceive
No change in your condition;
Though they cut away
Half your corporal channel
You remain the same You,
Solid in your nurturing sparkle,
Fluid in your sharing soul.

HEARING LOSS

It has become all too clear
Audible signals are disappearing;
I am missing the balm of your laughter,
There is pain losing the sound of your breath.

When a treasure starts to fade,
What remains becomes even more cherished;
A prudent man becomes more attentive,
Takes steps to reduce the depth of his loss.

Hearing less, I must see more,
Watching truth in the movement of your lips
Reading your mood from the width of your smile
Knowing your love from the tilt of your chin.

WHEN YOU ARE AWAY

It should be cold when you are away,
Your absence hammering ice through my veins,
Draining the fluid from my essence
Like the sting of the knifing westerly wind.

Instead it is blisteringly hot,
The sweating air mirroring my distress,
Pressing against its haze, not letting
Breath escape by so much as a single sigh.

In anxiety for your return
The sunshine exhausts its dynamic core,
Pouring its frenzied wave in one line
Direct to the bold crush of the frightened fold.

TO MERGE WITH EARTH

Blue but threatening, the schizoid sky
Tramples its horizon,
As though to merge with earth,
Blend with placid waters
For one monochromatic vista.

Perfect solitude, marauding hopes
Nourish such compulsion;
Time is a healing splint,
Yet slow for some fractures,
And even the sky can be lonely.

JANUARY BY THE LAKE

Wide barometric swings
Are the fashion here.
The sun spills its gold-dust
And melting ice murmurs
Its appreciation;
But the gratitude is all too brief
For celestial largesse knows limits
And before the afternoon is spent
The sun has sped to
Other indigent quarters.
Frost again asserts dominion,
Pressing more gently this time, knowing
Its potency is temporal,
Its season's quickly drawn;
Such is the nature of this place that
Cold cannot long rule our hearts.

SPIRIT OF THE INLAND SEA

Through the wintry incomplete apocalypse
It hovered low and froze
In rough disjointed ripples,
Powerless to shape the dunes
More swollen years can summon.

Past the standard march of seasonal turnstiles
This spring it hushed its hum
And played in pools with rattles,
Like shale sliding down a trough
To sound no rousing signal.

In the blistered wake of stinging summer rain
Its level rose and splashed
In drunken glee with vengeance,
Bubbling toward the upper stretch
Of pseudo-tidal reaches.

Now it tips against the beach of warm repose
The waft of liquid life
Confirmed though shrunk in body,
Ebbing, ready to attain
Freshwater ocean's essence.

LULLABY FOR MY LOVER

Sleep and dream of peace,
I will guard your night,
And when the daybreak brings another
                                      gentle breeze,
He will show you light.

Though you love, you seek
The fire at the source,
The reasons pain and grief exist, and why it seems
Wisdom yields to force.

Questions born of love,
Questions from the heart,
Ask — the answers you will learn in time, but do not
Question where to start.

Darkness shrouds with war,
Blinds us with its blight;
Make your eyes discern the shades of glory looming
Waiting for the light.

Sleep and dream of light,
While I guard your night,
When with the daybreak comes another
                                      gentle breeze,
He will bring you peace.

IMAGE

Created in the image —
In some ways like,
In more ways unlike
The One, The All-Encompassing Original.

A shining surface oft distorts
The form it strives to show
And makes the picture most dissimilar;
So mankind a most imperfect image is,
Maladroit, moving in clumsy natures
Through an unfamiliar milieu,
Taking uneven steps,
Stumbling in a semi-darkness of
Eyes half-closed toward The Original,
Confusing the reflection
And throwing back vice, greed, corruption —
A plethora of wrongs.

But even the poorest image
Contains some glimmer of the best from its original,
And within the frame of each of us
Some good glints through.
Anyone who stands before a mirror
Can improve his likeness
By the mere suggestion of a smile,
As though his very spirit
Could be transported across the air
And imbue the lifeless glass with feeling;
How much more powerful
Are the beams of Him
Who smiles on all,
Who transmits His love to His each and every image
Aiding and exhorting it
To be better than it was.

THIS TIME

This time
The resolution shall not melt in
the morning aftermath;
This time
The purpose shall not be stayed by a
thousand after-doubts;
This time
The clear course charted in thorough
planning will be kept;
This time
There will be no waiting for "next time":
This time is The Time.

THREE FALLS

A man drowning in the tears of angels
Plods with his cross-grained burden
And sees all life before him,
Sees again the tribute brought,
Brought to the cradled king –

Gold for the love of light,
The spirit of valued insight
And the sparkle in living minds;

Frankincense for the burning glory,
The fragrance of heaven brought close,
The scent that can quicken the heart;

Myrrh for the birth that follows death,
The balm that perfumes and preserves,
Myrrh for the healing of souls.

A king flowing in blood from the crown
Cushions the earth as he falls –
One fall for the gold
One fall for the frankincense
One fall for the myrrh.

A son pouring wine for the saints
Waits for the goblet's rising –
The first day for the myrrh
The second day for the frankincense
The third day for the gold.

LIGHTEN OUR DARKNESS

Only within darkness can light be discerned
While the gaze is limited by lenses filmed,
Receptors puffy from the burden of dust;
Twilit cells to splendour ploddingly are turned.

Darkness cannot be deciphered without light,
Be it by glowing lamp as pupils expand
Or groping fingers making tentative touch;
Truth will penetrate by feel if not by sight.

PERILS AND DANGERS

"Give us back the night," she demanded,
As though we owned it —
As though we had ever owned it.

From earliest times
We sought refuge from its blackness,
We trapped fire and cast it back
To block advance of darkness,
We barred the doors and closely drew the curtains
To keep its evil spirits from our homes.

The watchman on his wary round
Knows the dangers of the night;
He steps with measured care toward corners,
Through foreign dark he guardedly approaches,
Delegate from proprietors diurnal,
Envoy to the savage midnight shades.

Though we at times do chance a streetlamp journey,
We dare not fail to move with senses primed,
Or pausing, rest alert
For sudden peril;
Evil knows no single class of victim,
Its agents strike at targets everywhere.

Moonlight rituals
Yield joys not savoured free of risk;
Nature plays a wayward part —
It swamps in cloudy reason
Minds once untouched, healthy; and then becomes
A human soul a creature of the dark.

Many wild fears and murky shadows
Must be defeated
Before we can reclaim the night.

THIS NIGHT

There are no moon and stars tonight,
Some lover gave them all away;
His lady owns them and his life —
Once more the sky's in disarray.

There have been many darkened nights
When trysts have beckoned trusting gifts;
Generous souls have braved their scope
And opened astronomic rifts.

On this and every black-crowned night
Old promises are framed anew,
And sometimes darkness has prevailed
For not all pledges stand when due.

Celestial vows are smothered up
In jars of earth with lids of rue;
Though these absorb and douse the light,
A worthy heart knows what to do:

It grasps the proffered sparkling dream,
And then a larger version makes,
Restores the product to its source;
So love redeems what first it takes.

THE FEBRUARY 24th SLEEP EXPERIENCE

Total oblivion
Through half the night
In the cavernous depths
And airy passages
Of the fourth phase.
Then by way of counterbalance
A restless jumping back and forth
From another stage
Of light low voltage repose
Into the Rapid Eye Movements.
At first a rumbling
Like wheels of a distant trolley,
Gathering the drum of thunder,
Growing to explode, as ice will
When it breaks the eerie winter.
Frantic for a razor —
Scrambling, scrabbling
Must clear away the growth
And unmask
The human being beneath —
Scrambling, scrabbling
Now in an ancient wardrobe
Now in my parents' home —
Then you touch my face
And whisk away the beard.
Finally a river
Peaceful pure and soothing,
Knowing whom it seeks,
Powerful, life-giving,
Gentle in its course.
In the morning we trade remembrances
Of our slumberous ruminations and learn
Both dreamt the same dream.

MATCH

It seemed Satan was winning
the arm wrestling match;
By degrees just perceptible
his arm bore down,
And his followers' smiles
made the odds-makers frown.

Their faces impassive,
other onlookers stared,
Intent on the chalk-line
drawn near to the elbows,
Patiently waiting, watching
with eyes that won't close.

Satan's opponent
was quite evenly breathing,
A soft calm was concealing
the fire from his lungs,
The same fire known of old
to leap forth in bold tongues.

A young man turning on a lonely corner
Sees a beaten victim lie bleeding beyond;
A young man turning on a lonely corner
Hesitates, troubled — then runs to the aid of
The crumpled stranger in his crimson-stained pond.

And the clasped hands inched back
                            to equilibrium.

Manor House Publishing
(905) 648-2193

www.ingramcontent.com/pod-product-compliance
Lightning Source LLC
Chambersburg PA
CBHW031258290426
44109CB00012B/646